Happy Birthday Bob!

Richard Stockton

Fondle
The Fear

Fondle The Fear

… the funniest way
to turn your fear into power.

A Three-Step Method by
Richard Stockton

Great Press
3940 Laurel Canyon Blvd., Suite 635
Studio City, CA 91604

ISBN 0-9726166-0-8

LCCN 2002096124

Edited by Bobbie Christmas
Designed by Mark Hall
Cover and dancing man photographs by
Tom Abbott and Jeff Vavricka
Author Photograph by Sandy Spear

DEDICATION

This book is dedicated to you who
want to be someone.

It is also dedicated to you who want
to be someone else.

NOTE TO THE READER:

The stories in this book are true; the events happened and the people in them exist. I tell these stories to show you my journey to fondle the fear. The jokes in this book show how I reframe the fright.

ACKNOWLEDGMENTS

To those comics who helped me with material in this book, thanks to Steve Bruner, Darren Carter, Evan Davis, Phil The Security Guard, Paul Lyons, The Swami Beyondananda, Trudelight, Brad Upton, and Mike Welch.

I also want to thank all the fine comedians with whom I've spent thousands of hours discovering what is funny.

I'd like to give special thanks to my editor, Bobbie Christmas, for lessons in clarity.

I want to express my gratitude to Jan Stockton, Dirk Stockton and Sierra Stockton for their never-ending help and support.

Finally, I wish to acknowledge my brilliantly hilarious brother, Dan Stockton, who showed me how to laugh at the scariest things in life.

Contents

Fondle This First 13

Step One: Dream 23
- Anyone can be a Victim;
  Dream and be a Suspect
- Power Naps Power Dreams

Step Two: the Golden "Hey!" 49
- How to Use the Golden "Hey!"
- Five Golden "Hey!" Stories
- Suit up for Success
- Why Say "Hey!"
- Eat Your Words

Step Three: Fondle The Fear 79
- Fear
- Fear Mongers
- Fear Into Excitement
- The Power of Now
- The Power of Sooner or Later
- "Now Fear This!"
- Jump From The Frying Pan Into Desire

Bonus Chapter! 139

Index 145

fondle (fon´d'l)
1. gently caress

Webster's New World Dictionary

When animals escape an attack, they tremble and shake to release their fear. We have been conditioned to store trauma and have lost the ability to face our fears. When you sense that you've hidden fear in your body, fondle yourself.

Fondle This First

You can say,
"California public education is
forty-ninth in the nation,"
or
"Hey! Thank God for
Mississippi."

Richard Stockton

When you "fondle the fear," you embrace your fear and turn it into excitement. The difference between fear and excitement blew into my face in Texas.

I was in Lubbock, home of some of the fiercest storms in the world. I was staying at a motel with indoor/outdoor carpeting in the bathroom. My second story floor vibrated every time a cattle truck passed. I first noticed the wind when it began to whistle around the windows. A radio announcer warned that a tornado was headed straight for Lubbock. The motel walls started shaking, I turned on the TV. All the channels gave tornado advisories and told everyone to take cover. The electricity went out, and there was nothing but the howling wind and rattling walls. I wondered what to do in a tornado, "Stand in the doorway? No, that's an earthquake.

I pulled open the door an inch. A lawn chair blew by A garbage can shot past. I peered out into the street, and oh, my God, there was a kid out in the tornado. The kid was being blown down the street. The kid was . . . on a skateboard. He wore a huge grin, had his jacket pulled up over his head to catch the wind, and yelled, "Eeeeeeeeehaw!"

I shook; he sailed.
I hid from the wind; he embraced it.
I feared death; he had the time of his life.

You can say,
"I'm schizophrenic,"
or you can say,
"Hey! I'm beside myself."

Richard Stockton

Fear is most powerful
when lurking in the shadows.

One way to embrace your imagined fear is to experience fear of something that is truly dangerous. The first day I moved to Los Angeles, my head was full of frightening stories about mean city streets, and I imagined hoodlums waiting in the dark to jump me. During the early evening, I nervously scanned the want ads for a cheap room and found this ad under Rooms For Rent.

> BURBANK select area, priv. rm. and ba, priv. entrance, TV, refrig., $75 wk, (818) 300-3114

The ad sounded like a great deal, so I dialed the number.
"Hi, I'm calling about the room for rent."
"What about it?" Her whiskey voice barked like a dog.
"Is it still for rent?"
"Well, yeah. Listen, do you work?"
"Yes."
I was ignored as another woman yelled in the background, "Who the hell is that?"
"How do I know? Shut up."
She returned to me. "So what do you want?"
"Uh … there's a private entrance?"
"What? You want to go in there?"
"Yes. I'm looking for a place to live."
"Where do you live now?"
"I'm staying at the TraveLodge."
"That's expensive, boy. You'd better rent a goddamn room."
"That's why I called you."
"You called me? I don't even know you."
"My name is Richard Stockton. May I see the room?"

You can say,
"I'm locked up in jail,"
or
"Hey! I'm in a gated community."

Richard Stockton

"Well, you'll have to come here first. Why would anyone live in a hotel who's got a job?"

"I'm looking for a room."

"How about looking for a job?"

"I'm interested in your room."

"Well, you'll have to come see it first."

She gave me the address, and I found the old house in the dark. I walked to the front door and knocked, but the people inside shouted at each other so loudly they couldn't hear me. "Don't call him. If he wants to come, he'll come."

"You screwed it up. Where the hell is he?"

"Get away from that goddamn phone."

"Take your hands off me."

"Shut up, you bitch. I gave him directions."

They still couldn't hear me knock, so I went to the rear entrance. I banged loudly on the back door and saw a round, red form peer through the curtained window.

"Who is that?"

"Richard Stockton."

"What do you want?"

"I'm here to look at the room."

The door flew open. She had a bright red wig plastered down over her skull like a helmet. She was shaped like a pumpkin, in an orange jumpsuit with a green collar. An unlit, broken cigarette, covered with lipstick, dangled from the corner of her mouth. In her right hand, she held a meat cleaver.

"Have you got a job?"

"Yes, I work all the time. I'm a comedian."

"Ha, ha, very funny. What a joke. Where do you live?"

"I'm staying at the TraveLodge. May I see the room?"

She backed up and I stepped into the kitchen. She waved her meat cleaver behind her. "You gotta watch her. She's got Alzheimer's. She's asleep; don't go in there."

I kept my hand on the doorknob, poised for escape.

"Oh, Christ! You woke her up. Well, you can come in the goddamn door now. Stay out of the refrigerator."

You can say,
"They showed me the door,"
or
"Hey! An opening."

Richard Stockton

"But the ad said …"

She gripped the meat cleaver. "Don't you ever touch that refrigerator. Your bathroom is private. Once a day we all take showers in it."

"You will be showering in my bathroom?"

"We gotta get clean, don't we?"

An ancient woman in a sleeping gown that had once been white tottered out of the bedroom. Her long, white hair frizzled out two feet in all directions like she was in electroshock. Her chin nearly touched her nose, and she thrust her pursed face into mine. "Have you got a job?"

The pumpkin woman with the meat cleaver had closed the door behind me. I was surrounded. I faked a move to the refrigerator, and she threw her big, orange body against it.

"Don't touch it!"

I backpedaled to the door. "Thanks, but…" and I was outside in the cool, fresh LA November night. They yelled at each other as I backed away.

"Well, does he have a goddamn job?"

"Shut up. He's some kind of actor. How the hell should I know what he does?"

I walked out the driveway along the side of the house. A window flew open, and the pumpkin bellowed at me, "You didn't look at the room. You gotta look at the room."

I kept moving. She ran into the next room and threw open the window. "You can have it. It's yours."

I could see the street. I walked faster.

"Seventy-five dollars. Come back!"

I smiled as I stepped into the dark street. My encounter in the tiny room reframed my fear of mean city streets; hey, out on the street at night, you are invisible, and you can run.

Now fear did not lurk in the shadows; I was a shadow.

Step One:
Dream

Anyone Can Be A Victim; Dream And Be A Suspect

Power Naps Power Dreams

**If you expect to see yourself clearly,
then you must be out of your mind.**

You can say,
"I've been in this bank line forever,"
or
"Hey! I'm earning interest."

Richard Stockton

Anyone can be a Victim; Dream and be a Suspect

**If you're not living your dream
you're living someone else's.**

I felt manipulated even as I trudged into my bank, the papers covered with my identification numbers clutched in my sweaty fist. I stood in line behind a young woman with blue hair and in front of an elderly woman with blue hair. Every time someone finished at a window, the teller pressed a buzzer, and everyone dutifully moved up one step and stood until the buzzer sounded again. How humiliating to be programmed to move by a buzzer in a Pavlovian goose step. This situation was not my dream it was my nightmare. My brain short circuited. An electrical charge shot through my head. "Hey! My dream is to be in charge of my life."

Someone left a window. I heard the buzzer. As everyone in front of me took one conditioned step forward, I fondled the fear and I . . . stood still. I made it my dream. Imagine making a great American institution fit your dream.

I stood between the velvet ropes, and no one dared to circumvent the velvet ropes. I could hear the teeth grinding behind me. Someone left a window, and the buzzer sounded. I took a deep breath, fondled the fear and in one bold stroke, I stood still. Víva la revolución!

You can say,
"I lose six cents on
every book I sell,"
or
"Hey! Every time you don't buy
one, I make six cents."

Richard Stockton

The little blue-haired lady behind me poked me in the back with her pocketbook. "Move up. Move up, the line's supposed to move."

I turned to her. "Madam, will your turn come any sooner if you stand here, rather than there? Am I destroying your momentum? Were you on a roll?"

The bank security guard came over to me. Even as he set his recessive jaw and I set my recessive jaw, even as we stood eyeball to eyeball and I felt my contact lenses dry out, I stood fast. When he put his hand on his gun, I moved up; I'm not taking hot lead, and I would not advise that you do, either, but hey, I had become more than a number in a line. I was somebody he would shoot. I was worth a bullet.

> By obeying programmed commands,
> we think we're getting somewhere.

FONDLING THE FEAR

Here are three ways you can be worth a bullet.
- Serenade your girlfriend's dorm with a banjo.
- Walk a mile in someone else's shoes at a Japanese restaurant.
- Give party horns to kids at freeway rest areas.

All of us have pulled the covers over our heads. These FONDLING THE FEAR sections are about getting out from under the covers.

"There are no facts. There are only interpretations."

Frederick Nietzsche

"If at first you don't succeed, change your definition of success."

Richard Stockton

The Three-Step Method

I took charge of my life in the bank with these three steps.

Step One: Dream

In the middle of my nightmare, I remembered my dream: to be in charge of my own life. You went through 25,000 hours of conditioning by your parents. Conditioning controls everything but your hair. To overcome conditioning, you must know your dream. When Martin Luther King said, "I have a dream," he was not selling a mattress.

Step Two: The Golden "Hey!"

I used The Golden "Hey!" to seize the perspective of power in the bank line. At the golden moment, I said, "Hey, my dream is to be in charge of my life."
The disapproval behind me sounded bad so, hey, I changed the words. "*Víva la revolución!*"
The pressure looked bad, so, hey, I changed the picture. "I'm Gandhi with a PIN!"
Obeying the bank guard felt bad so, hey, I changed the meaning of the outcome. "I'm worth a bullet."

Step Three: Fondle The Fear

To paraphrase Franklin Delano Roosevelt, "We have nothing to fear but looking paranoid." Fear and excitement show up in your body the same way. The difference between fear and excitement is what you call it. When you resist it, it is fear. When you embrace it, it is excitement. I turned my fear of being controlled by the bank buzzer into excitement. I embraced the fear. I stood my ground. I froze.

You can say,
"Yes, you caught me
talking to myself,"
or
"Hey! I'm in a meeting here."

Richard Stockton

To get what you really want, you must first go into a dream state. You find yourself by leaving your conditioned brain.

If you expect to see yourself clearly, then you must be out of your head.

The best things in life are not things; they are your dreams, your excitement and your interpretation of it all. I've been listening to my own success tape since 1988.

- I've got something Bill Gates will never have, a woman who makes more money than I do.

- I am chauffeured in a $76,000 vehicle, a city bus. I network with people from thirteen countries.

- I truly am Rich; it's on my driver's license.

One thing is certain, your power lies in believing in your dream.

You can be someone.
You can even be someone else.

You can say,
"Manic depression
is killing me,"
or
"Hey! Mania gives me exercise,
depression gives me the extra
sleep I need."

Richard Stockton

You find yourself by dreaming. You can't look for your dream, because it would be like looking for your glasses. The thing you need to find is the thing you need to find them with, like a deaf guy trying to find his hearing aid with a clapper. Dream on.

Your dream may be no further than your own backyard, especially if you have a hammock. Dream your dream. Start now; take a nap. My most creative moments are when waking up from a nap. Nap on the job and it's a "power nap." Power naps power dreams.

FONDLING THE FEAR

Did you want to be a fireman but grow up to be merely an arsonist? Do both. You're a self-starter. Set the world on fire.

How do you go into a dream state?

- Get a slower modem.

- Go to Kinko's with a question.

- Ask your husband how he feels.

You can say,
"I hate junk mail,"
or
"Hey! I've got a belly full of
Spam."

Richard Stockton

If you're not following your dream, then you're following someone else's.

An agent called me with an audition for a Visa commercial. "You're exactly what they're looking for."

"Is there a script, or is it improv?"

"Uh, I don't know. We didn't get copy."

"If you didn't get copy, how do you know I'm exactly what they're looking for?"

"Well . . . they're looking . . . for a Seinfeld."

"I'm nothing like Seinfeld. Maybe Kramer, but not Seinfeld."

"That's it! Kramer. You're perfect."

"Look, it takes an entire day to drive into Hollywood, audition, and sit through commuter traffic home. I've got to be sure that I've got a chance."

"You do. You're exactly what they're looking for. It's, well, it's my first day here, and Mickey told me to call you, and . . ."

"Mickey gave you my number? Thanks, but no thanks."

"You've got to go. My God, it's a national TV commercial. They want . . . they want a Kramer type. I know they do. This is a big break for you. They want someone funny."

I knew the trip would waste my day, but the thought of the money from a Visa commercial clouded my mind. There were fifty more productive things I could have done, but I said, "OK."

I used hot curlers and gel to get my hair up, and I wore a long john to look lanky like Kramer. I had to park six blocks from the casting office. I ran all the way, burst into the waiting room, and was surrounded by middle-aged fat guys. They were so fat I felt like I was floating in flesh.

You can say,
"I'm getting fat,"
or
"Hey! I'm beating anorexia."

Richard Stockton

I got the script; it was about fat guys riding exercise bikes who decide to use their Visa cards to buy real bicycles. My audition line was for Guy #3. "We don't want to look at reflections of our spare tires." I did not have a spare tire, and I would have done better asking for spare change.

I practiced my line in the waiting room with twenty guys who had spare tires to spare, guys who carried Hefty Bag lunches. They waved their sandwiches in my face while they taunted me.

"Look at Mr. Skinny trying to stick out his poor little belly."

"Eat a Twinkie, Swizzle Stick."

"Who invited Bony Morony?"

I was hardly skinny, but next to these guys, I looked anorexic. My reading was with a black Santa Claus type who jeered at me. "See man, I've got the form they want." He raised his huge belly, dropped it, and it bounced three times

In a sweat, I stood on my mark beside the big, round man. The casting director frowned at me, shook his head, and said, "Rolling." My line was the last in the scene. I said, "We don't want to look at reflections of our spare tires," and stuck out my belly. Then my huge partner swung his belly sideways with both hands, like a wrecking ball, and clobbered me. The blow knocked me off my feet and out of the picture frame. The camera continued to video the big round guy laughing, and rubbing his amazing belly.

He was right about his form; later I saw him on TV in the Visa commercial, pedaling an exercise bike, saying, "We don't want to look at reflections of our spare tires." It must have been his dream.

You can say,
"These blinds are filthy,"
or
"Hey! Earth tones."

Richard Stockton

FONDLING THE
THERMAL BUTTER BOX

When I moved from my car into my studio apartment, it was suggested that I needed a refrigerator, so I went to an appliance store, and the salesman insisted that I buy one that had a thermal butter box to keep the butter from getting hard in the refrigerator. He pressed his sweaty face close to mine. "You don't want to have someone over for dinner and serve hard butter, do you?"

My head spun. I thought, "Wait a minute, it is cold outside, so I buy an insulated house that I pay to heat. Then I buy a refrigerator to protect my food from the heat I paid for. Now I am told that I need to buy a refrigerator with a thermal butter box to protect my butter from the cold I paid for in the refrigerator!"

What if you were caught between rock-hard butter and a cold place? You dream of having soft butter, so how could you:

1) be warm
2) keep your food cool
3) serve soft butter?

Fondle the fear and get close to the hard butter. What makes the butter hard? The refrigerator. I didn't buy one. As I pumped the salesman's hand, I thanked him for showing me how to have it all. I keep my food out on the porch, my butter and my body inside the house. To this day, I'm warm, my food is cool, and I have soft butter. Imagine how I impress my dinner guests!

You can say,
"I dreamed of being an artist
but grew up to be merely a
counterfeiter,"
or
"Hey! How many artists
actually make money?"

Richard Stockton

Your dreams will tell you who you are, so you can use the power of perspective to fondle any fear.

I could say, "I never finish anything," or "Hey, I attended four colleges in less than two years . . . Renaissance Man."

Living with no dream devastated my life. I had all the necessary ingredients for instant, absolute power; everything but a dream. I had convictions but only misdemeanors. I had no focus and even when I got contact lenses, I wore them swimming, opened my eyes underwater, and watched them float away. I had no vision. How did I find out what I really wanted? In despair I laid down, fell into a deep sleep, and dreamed that I was at The Last Supper. No, I was not one of the twelve disciples,* but the caterer. I am here on earth not to heal, but offer a new menu of possibilities.

A woman said to me, "I can't have a dream, I'm a housewife." I told her, "You can have a dream. Instead of being a housewife, hey, you could be a man's wife."

To the approval-seeking rebel, to the impatient procrastinator, dream on!

Think of the Three Steps as the three wheels of your Golden Tricycle. Once you take Step One and dream you will have the front wheel of The Golden Tricycle, the wheel that determines your direction. The other two wheels will follow.

---

* Not one of the disciples was named Rich.

You can say,
"I'm stuck on a cruise
ship with doctors and lawyers,"
or
"Hey! It'll make the
vacation seem longer."

Richard Stockton

You gotta tell Santa what you want for Christmas, or you'll get fruitcake.

You gotta tell Amtrak where you're going, or they'll put you off in Bakersfield.

FONDLING THE FEAR

Make your dreams work for you.

Narcoleptic's Dream

Your dream is to be able to hold a job and still doze. You can really live your dream. You are a Power Nap consultant. You are the Master Napster. You travel around the world, dozing off with CEOs, presidents, and spiritual leaders.

Claustrophobic's Dream

Your dream is to enjoy tight places, and your fear is that you will be put in a straightjacket. Fondle yourself in that straightjacket. You're not trapped in a straightjacket; you're giving yourself a big hug.

You can say,
"People go on missions
merely to deliver Awake
Magazine,"
or
"Hey! The Jehovah's
Witness Protection Program."

Richard Stockton

Power Naps Power Dreams

You have infinite possibilities even if you dream of something as illusive as fame. In the Guinness Book of World Records 2000 Amar Bharti of India became famous for holding his arm up for twenty-six years. Now he can dream big, BOTH ARMS UP!

The Guinness Book of World Records is a dream catalogue for being famous. Guinness is also the name of a famous beer. Coincidence?

FONDLING THE FEAR

You can dream of being famous in The Guinness Book of World Records. Do extended periods of catatonia dash your dreams for fame? Fall into your dream state and break the record for standing motionless; eighteen hours, six minutes. You can succeed in your sleep with my method.

When you know what you want, you will find it. Look behind the couch.

You can say,
"With this remote and 124 TV
channels, I'm catatonic,"
or,
"Hey! Thumbs of steel."

Richard Stockton

Fondle #1

Make a list of

1) My inner heartfelt dreams and aspirations:

_____

2) Cool stuff I've seen on TV:

_____

_____

_____

_____

_____

_____

_____

_____

_____

_____

_____

_____

_____

_____

Step Two:
The Golden "Hey!"

How To Use The Golden "Hey!"
Five Golden "Hey!" Stories
Suit Up For Success
Why Say "Hey!"
Eat Your Words

Who was the greatest clutch baseball player of all time, the guy who would turn it around when the game seemed lost?   — Willie Mays, "The Say Hey Kid."

You can say,
"Marriage made me crazy,"
or
"Hey! Marriage got me
into therapy."

Richard Stockton

How To Use The Golden "Hey!"

We all want to look at our situations in a positive light, because deep down, we all know we must, to get the best results, to go the farthest, to climb the highest. How can you shine your positive light on dim doings? I present the most powerful tool ever developed by man, The Golden "Hey!"

If the words that describe your situation sound bad to you, say, "Hey!" and change the words.

Look for the benefit in your situation. When you're thirsty and have no water say, "Hey! I'm ninety-two percent water. Lucky I haven't drowned."

You're not just small potatoes; hey, you're new potatoes.

You can also use "Hey!" to seize an opportunity.

You can say, "My wife is in bed with another man," or "Hey! New pants."

Always reword your challenge so it is an asset.

"A thick wallet ruined my spine, but hey! A doctor removed all the cash."

You already know how to dream. Use The Golden "Hey!" to fondle the fear and turn fear into excitement.

- Instead of saying, "I'm fired," say, "Hey! Quality time with my dog."

- Instead of saying, "Root canal," say, "Hey! Nitrous oxide opportunity."

You can say, "I'm locked
away in this prison,"
or
"Hey! I'll never lose my
keys."

Richard Stockton

FONDLING THE FEAR

Imagine you are serving a prison sentence. Find ways to see how your "time" benefits you.

- Free conference calls

- No grocery shopping

- No commute

- All the time in the world

- No bills to pay

- Free haircuts

- You always know what to wear

- Free wake-up calls

You can say,
"I don't have any
computer games,"
or
"Hey! I can use my backspace
key to simulate Pac Man."

Richard Stockton

FONDLING THE FEAR

While money isn't everything, believing in the resources you have will make you more powerful. Use The Golden "Hey!" to feel your possibilities.

- You want a bigger house?
  Get smaller furniture.

- A room is too small for a bean bag chair?
  Get a Hacky Sack.

- Tired of your wimpy speakers?
  Listen to Windham Hill.

- You want to feel richer?
  Move into a cheaper house

In Los Angeles the highways have shoulder bumps to warn you when your tires are on the edge. When I moved to the mountains, the roads had no bumps and I wondered, "How do you know when you're too close? Then I noticed, "Hey! Trees."

Using The Golden "Hey!" is fondling the fear in the face of irrefutable facts.

You can say,
"It's just one thing
after another,"
or
"Hey! A parade."

Richard Stockton

Five Golden "Hey!" Stories

I

Use The Golden "Hey!" on your problems (fears) to find the positive possibility with every event in your life. In this first story, I fondled a frustrating traffic jam until I realized a career dream.

It's my first day in my new Los Angeles apartment and I'm trying to return to my new place. A cop stops me at the end of my street to explain that The Rose Parade will block the street, and I'd better head north. I fight through traffic and try to turn onto my street, when a cop yells, "Move on! If you turn, I've got to arrest you. The parade is still in progress."

The parade was still in progress. Hey, a dream opportunity!

Suddenly there I am on national TV, millions of people watching me slowly drive by, waving my hand to those on the sidewalk. My friends, family members, and millions of Americans are at home watching me being adored by the crowd, along with high school marching bands of massive tuba players with big red circles painted on their cheeks, floats of commercial actors, a championship bowling team and an actress waving her legs that were insured for a million dollars in 1953. I'm floating!

I came to Los Angeles to make it in show business and by using The Golden "Hey!" my first day, I'm in The Rose Parade. OK, the police gave me a $500 fine for crashing the parade, but hey! It's an entrance fee.

You can say,
"He's a kleptomaniac,"
or
"Hey! Extreme self-help."

Richard Stockton

II

Use The Golden "Hey!" to change the words when you're busted.

I was five when my mother walked into the kitchen and gasped to see my hand in the cookie jar.

"Dick! What are you doing?"

"Counting the cookies."

If you don't like the sound of your situation, make it sound different.

III

In Los Angeles, people will steal anything. Mark loved his Scottish terrier and kept it in his one-bedroom apartment. After it had been sprayed point blank by a skunk, Mark was unable to stand the dog inside his apartment and he let the loud animal out. We happened to glance out his window just as a van stopped, a young man grabbed the dog, and hopped back into the car with the animal. Mark ran outside, and the car took off. One half block later, it screeched to a halt, the window rolled down, and the dog came flying out.

As Mark nuzzled the reeking animal, he said, "Hey! Thank God for skunks."

IV

I was new to Hollywood, very anxious and depressed about having no prospects, when the phone rang. See how I turned this call into an affirmation of my dream of working in show business.

It was a woman with a Hungarian accent.

"Reechard?"

"Yes."

"Do you a-streep?"

You can say,
"I have no shower,"
or
"Hey! I'm so French."

Richard Stockton

"Excuse me?"

"Do you a-steeeep, you know, singing telegram?"

"No."

"Cause I know you are a comic, and comics don't make much money, and you could make forty dollars plus tips, if you a-streep. Do you have a belly?"

"No."

"Are you a white guy?"

"Who are you?"

"Do you have a tan?"

"How did you get my number?"

"Cause if you are a white guy, you got to have a tan. You could go to the beach, or for seven dollars you can get a tan at a salon. Is good investment."

"Do you hire comics?"

"Once in a blue moon, but if you a-streep, you have to be trained."

"Trained?"

"You need a tuxedo or a gorilla suit, but don't expect to get lucky."

"Get lucky? With a gorilla?"

"Men want to do it all the time, always ready. The girls I send out get offers but not so often the males. I have heard stories, though, wow! Yeah, women telling you to come back later, but don't expect to get lucky."

"I don't feel lucky."

"You want to make it in this business, you have to prepare. Mark didn't know nothing, and now he does it all the time."

"You got my number from Mark?"

"Uh-oh, my line is ringing. Ciao." (dial tone)

Dazed, I hung up the phone and then realized, "Hey, all I need to get work in Hollywood is a tan and a gorilla suit. Also, what great preparation for the next Planet of The Apes casting call!"

You can say,
"She's like living
with The Three Faces of Eve,"
or
"Hey! How about those
six legs of Eve!"

Richard Stockton

V

Reframing powerlessness starts by find the sweet spot of your nightmare.

I got on a Monday morning bus and sat behind two young, long-haired teenage boys who were riding to school. The despair their journey caused them had pushed them low into their seats, and though they were clearly friends, their gloom made it hard for them to speak. Finally, one turned to the other.

"What did you do this weekend?"

"Dude. I got busted by the cops for smoking pot, dude."

"Dude. I got busted for vandalizing a police car."

His friend sat straight up, his voice quivered with excitement and his eyes sparkled.

"When did you get busted?"

"Friday night."

"Dude. I heard about you on the police radio when I was locked up in the patrol car!"

"That was you getting busted for pot? I listened to your bust too. Sweet, dude."

"Awesome, dude!"

"Totally awesome, dude!"

A cloud of confidence settled over these two young rebels, and I noticed that they sat straight and tall, while pride filled their beaming smiles.

Their fear was powerlessness. What could make a young man raging against the machine feel stronger, than to throw himself into the teeth of that machine, and find out that his best friend listened to the event on a police radio? Sweet,dude.

You can say,
"Every day is a
bad hair day,"
or
"Hey! I'm an Einstein."

Richard Stockton

Suit Up For Success

Why do I constantly wear this suit?
Why is this one suit the only clothing
I have?

When I'm out on a lecture tour, I wake up and see this suit in the rearview mirror, and I say, "Hey, that's me in that power tie." As I walk across the parking lot into the Starbucks restroom to shave and sponge bath, I'm dressed to impress myself, and I'm ready to pursue my dream.

FONDLING THE FEAR

What apparel might help you shatter the rules of conformity so you can seize an opportunity?

- Swim fins?

- A sombrero?

- Earmuffs and a shower cap?

- A brassiere worn on the outside of your blouse?

When you feel desperate,
why not walk into the office
dressed like a desperado?

You can say,
"Divorce ruined me,"
or
"Hey! It got me out of
real estate."

Richard Stockton

Why Say "Hey!"

Say "Hey!" in that space between stimulus and response to reroute the neural pathways in your brain. Ride over the weeds of fear that block your path and design your own road. The Golden "Hey!" is the Weed Whacker to freedom. Your brain is open to all the possibilities for you to realize your dream.

What you "Hey!" is what you get.

Say "Hey!" and describe your circumstances in a way that gives you instant power. Say "Hey!" and make sure your interpretation of events gives you something positive. If the words that describe your situation sound bad to you, change the words. Saying that your brown yard is California natural can open up ideas for your landscape. "Wow, are these rocks real?"

When you say "Hey!" you will see the possibilities after doing absolutely nothing. You are a success in spite of all the evidence. Who needs evidence? The police.

You can say,
"I've never been so
insulted in all my life,"
or
"Hey! I'm beginning to
appreciate the old insults."

Richard Stockton

Ninety percent of the words you say today, you will say tomorrow. By repeating words of fear over and over, you build neural freeways in your brain that make self-destructive behavior automatic. I went to my grammar school reunion and saw nine of my friends whose words as children crippled them as adults.

Nine Secrets of Nine People Nine Years Old

Tommy Harper always said, "Give me money." Today he is homeless.

George Burton said, "I didn't do it." He had just come from his bail hearing.

Sally Flynn said, "I hate baths." She married a Frenchman.

Bernard Goldberg asked, "Does this hurt?" He works for the IRS.

Donny Tribble shouted, "Spit wads!" He develops germ warfare.

Sean Coreman always asked, "Are we there yet?" He lives for the weekend.

Laurie Butell always said, "Oops." She sells insurance.

Marvin Williams always said, "I'm gonna be sick." He's a critic.

Bill Loden said, "I dare you to jump off the roof." Motivational speaker.

You can say that your head is half empty or that it is half full.

Richard Stockton

Eat Your Words

How many times have you heard, "You are what you eat?" On the self-image level, you are what you say you eat.

Saying "I eat hot dogs," says you go to sporting events.
Saying "I eat pig lips," says you go to your front yard for spare auto parts.

Saying "I eat sushi," says you serve hip food.
Saying "I eat raw fish," says you served in Laos.

Saying "I eat All-Bran," says you choose a healthy lifestyle.
Saying "I eat laxatives," says you choose not to bungee.

Saying "I eat sun-dried tomatoes," says you shop in a gourmet department.
Saying "I eat dehydrated vegetables," says you shop in a dumpster.

Saying "I eat filet mignon," says you fill your life with the best.
Saying "I eat dead cow," says you fill your life with flies.

When an old tape plays in your head, say,
"Hey!" and tape over it.

You can say,
"I've got a
drinking problem,"
or
"Hey! I've got a
drinking challenge."

Richard Stockton

Framing an event by calling it a problem solidifies the difficulty. Reframing it as a challenge makes the situation more like an experiment or, even a romantic test. Imagine if Robin Hood and Little John had met on the bridge and presented each other with a "problem." We'd have never heard of them. Imagine if Pepsi Cola had mounted an ad campaign where it tried to get people to take "The Pepsi Problem." Who wants to taste a problem?

You can say,
"I scored a basket for the other team,"
or
"Hey! I'm dangerous at both ends of the court."

Richard Stockton

Everything you say comes true, because your unconscious mind takes everything it hears literally.

• In "Jailhouse Rock" Elvis sang, "If you can't find a partner, use a wooden chair." He programmed an entire generation to love furniture.

• If you chant every day, "I will have an out-of-body experience," eventually you will have a baby, or you will puke, or both.

• Repeatedly say, "I will be channeling this year," and December may find you swimming from England to France.

FONDLING THE FEAR

When you use a cliché about yourself, be careful that your body does not interpret the cliché literally.

"I can't handle it." Hey, get unbreakable dishes.

"I got up on the wrong side of bed." Be careful putting on your wife's clothing.

"I could run circles around him." Resist the urge to jog around his cubicle.

"I can see the handwriting on the wall." Slow down; you're in the men's room.

"I can't get it through my head." Careful with those Q-tips!

You can say,
"My pickup has a ton of
chicken manure in back,"
or
"Hey! The weight makes it ride
smooth as a Cadillac."

Richard Stockton

Fondle #2

For each situation, choose the response that gives you the most power.

At times you want to turn around, pack it up and call it quits.

1) Before packing, take a nap. After being refreshed, you may decide that trying again is easier than packing.

2) Have good luggage.

Someone threw cold water on your idea.

1) You say, "It won't shrink."

2) You say, "Maybe I should not have set the model on fire."

Step Three:
Fondle the Fear

Fear
Fear Mongers
Fear Into Excitement
The Power of Now
The Power of Sooner or Later
"Now Fear This!"
Jump From the Frying Pan Into Desire

Fear is powerful when lurking in the shadows. The unknown is what is scary. The movie, "The Blair Witch Project" scared people because nobody knew what it was about. Men fear kegels because men don't know when they are happening.

You can say,
"I'm being stalked,"
or
"Hey! Extreme dating."

Richard Stockton

Fear

You can let fear freeze your spirit or you can embrace it, fondle it; then that feeling becomes excitement and you are free to be on your way. That's why it's called a freeway.

The sensation of "fear" and "excitement" are the same. The only difference is what you call it. Every time Goofy goes over a cliff, what does he say? "Ya-ha-hooie-hooie!" He just turned fear into excitement. Imagine you're running full speed and you trip, even as you're diving headfirst over concrete try thinking, "Hey, I'm flying." You focus on the thrill of flying and your body gets ready to tuck and roll. Falling is an opportunity to fly. The road will rise to meet you.

The difference between sideswiping a parked car and driving in the Indy 500 is the look on the driver's face, and the Indy 500 has sponsors. If you're afraid of your own driving, get a helmet and turn your grimace to grin.

I can be positive even though my blood type is B negative.

You can say,
"I hit the wall,"
or
"Hey! I tied the record
for quickest stop."

Richard Stockton

First, name your fear and ask yourself, "What is the worst thing that can happen?" Now you've identified your deepest fear, a well of opportunity. Next, fondle the fear. Listen to the words. Feel it. Smell it. You're not scared, you're fondling your fear.

- "Oh, no!" becomes "Oh, boy!"

- "I have nothing to wear," becomes "Let's get naked!"

- "Somebody stop him!" becomes "Look at him go!"

- When you hit the wall, "Hey, flatter abs!"

I always wanted to be an evangelist healer but I had no faith. Now I ask people for money who are well.

Change is the way of all things, except from vending machines. Learn to fondle change, then wash your hands.

You can say,
"Killer bees. Giant asteroids.
How could it get any scarier?"
or
"Hey! Y3K!"

Richard Stockton

Fear Mongers

"The Justice Department has issued a blanket alert, in recognition of a general threat."
George W. Bush

"We should once again place the public on alert. The information we have does not point to any specific target ... and it does not outline any specific type of attack."
Tom Ridge, Homeland Security Director

"I believe it's called The Boogeyman."
Richard Stockton

The best way to fondle fear that is broadcast by politicians is to laugh at these fear mongers. The trick is to see them as the joke. George W. Bush is a perfect example of someone who is committed to spreading fear, and instead spreads laughter.

"I also made it clear to [Vladimir Putin] that it's important to think beyond the old days of when we had the concept that if we blew each other up, the world would be safe."
George W. Bush, Washington, D.C., May 1, 2001

"For every fatal shooting, there were roughly three non-fatal shootings. And, folks, this is unacceptable in America. It's just unacceptable. And we're going to do something about it."
George W. Bush, Philadelphia, May 14, 2001

Apparently Mr. Bush is for gun control with a tripod and a scope.

You can say,
"I got hit with a ton of bricks,"
or
"Hey! I've got a ton of bricks."

Richard Stockton

Fear Into Excitement

I learned to turn fear into excitement in the sixth grade. We had spent our childhood in the cold war. The cloud of nuclear doom hung over us until the day we raised the stakes and turned our fear into excitement. We lived in Sacramento, which thrived on military bases and missile factories, so we knew the Russians were going to annihilate us first. My mom stocked our basement with "bomb food." By surrendering to the possibility of our tragic demise at the hands of an evil empire, our lives began to sparkle. We were ground zero. It felt cool to potentially be dead heroes.

The Merrimont Elementary School lunch bell rang, and we ran out onto the dirt playground. Johnny Vanzelli spread out his map of Sacramento, and with red pens, we circled the air bases, the missile factories, and the munitions dump. We drew lines between the sites, and as we had suspected, they intersected on the tiny pink square that was our school. We were the perfect target for the first Russian nuclear attack. Johnny peered at the map. "Hold it. McClellan Air Force Base keeps our bombers, so the Russians will strike more to the east." He pointed at the side of the pink square. "That would put the target . . ." He stood, looked at the sun, walked twenty paces toward the baseball diamond, and shouted, "Right here!" He picked up a sharp rock and drew a big X in the dirt. It's one thing to hide under your desk in air raid drills, but that X was really IT. We had found the strategic center of the modern world, and it was us. This new perspective meant that in detention, we were being used as human shields. When we observed that the teacher was the only one with a metal desk to hide under, we cut school for our own survival.

You can say, "They're putting words in my mouth," or "Hey! Karaoke."

Richard Stockton

Fear of aging starts when you're told to be afraid of your age.

My father often told me, "You're not getting any younger." The first time he told me I was not getting any younger, I was twelve.

I paced the floor of my room. "Dad is right; I am not getting any younger, I'm going to be thirteen. It's gone by so fast; I have my first zit, my Little League career is over, girls look good to me, and I need to show ID to get my movie discount. They're going to take my braces off, the Mickey Mouse Club doesn't make sense anymore, and I can't remember the last time Mom took me into the Women's Room. I'm over the hill; body hair, voice cracks, a relentless erection, all part of the change of life; pubeopause. I'm a spotty banana. Twelve years; where did it all go?"

Fondle this fear; does it really make sense to be afraid of "not getting any younger?" Must I strive to get younger? That would be like living in reverse. I would have to forget how to tie my shoes and put them on the wrong feet. I would have to lose my permanent teeth, buy back my baby teeth one at a time with quarters, lose those teeth, and gum grownup fingers. I'd have to fall out of bed, crawl into a crib, and finally slide back into Mom. Getting older is confusing enough; I'm not up to getting younger.

Are you afraid of the anger and violence at today's rock concerts? I was, until I fondled the fear and went to see a rock concert with my fourteen-year-old son. I became so excited I rushed to the mosh pit like everyone else. I was a teenager again. The next day, my chiropractor recommended Steely Dan.

You can say,
"My husband never stops to ask
for directions,"
or
"Hey! My man goes
the extra mile."

Richard Stockton

Sometimes the best thing to do is to relax and enjoy the ride.

In a Detroit blizzard at six in the morning I got in a cab bound for the airport. The driver was a dark, thin Indian man crouched over the steering wheel like a bird. He had an enormous grin, and his black eyes twinkled. "You will arrive to the airport on time. Yes? Ha, ha."

He stomped on the gas, his tires spun on the deep snow, grabbed, and we rocketed between cars with inches on each side. He was completely relaxed and perfectly executed the most terrifying moves with a smile of beatitude. He was like Mario Andretti in Gandhi's body. The car spun out on some ice. We were sliding sideways, and he looked at me with genuine concern. "Is my driving pleasing you?" I could not breathe, let alone speak, and he gazed back at the road. "Is good you are not frightened of my driving."

We came to a steep hill and could see cars fishtail into one another ahead. He gunned the motor, cranked the wheel, and did a perfect one hundred eighty-degree spin. As his tires slid over the packed snow, he shifted into reverse, maintained his momentum, and continued up the hill backwards, passing the other cars. "Front-wheel drive most useful. Ha, ha."

I was twenty minutes early to the airport. As I paid my enthusiastic driver, he grabbed my hand and pressed my knuckles to his forehead. "I pray your journey will be safe."

"Thanks; I was doing that myself."

I stepped out of the car, my shoes lost their grip on the ice. I did the slow splits, and I went down on my butt.

The window rolled down, "See? Already you have made safe landing. Ha, ha." His tires spun over the ice. He perfectly timed the narrow space between a speeding bus and a sliding truck, he raised his thin arm out of the window, and waved good-bye.

You can say,
"I rob savings and loans,"
or
"Hey! I work banker's hours."

Richard Stockton

The more you embrace what you are afraid of, the more power you have.

In February of 1989, on my way to a gig at Laugh's Unlimited in Old Sacramento, I was arrested and charged with seven counts of armed robbery. I made it all the way through hard lockup before the cops realized they had the wrong guy.

Before receiving my jail uniform and going through a body-cavity search, I sat in the tank in my silk jacket and stage makeup. I did not look like the other men in the cell. I was packed into a tiny holding room with thirty men waiting to be processed for crimes ranging from indecent exposure to first-degree murder. My deepest fear was that I might look exactly like the guy who did the seven robberies, in which case I would do a stretch in prison.

A six-foot, eight-inch leather-clad man with a shaved head and a swastika tattooed on his face stepped in front of me, sneered, and snatched my arrest sheet from my hand. In jail, this behavior was tantamount to calling me "bitch." The crowded cell fell absolutely quiet. The giant slowly moved his lips as he read the facts of my arrest. His jaw dropped. "Armed robbery? You?"

The entire cell murmured with astonished admiration. The behemoth scanned my sheet.

"Seven times? You committed armed robbery seven times?"

I casually took back my arrest sheet and shrugged. "Who keeps count?"

For the remainder of my stay in jail, I was a respected man with clout. By embracing my deepest fear, the fear that people would think that I was an armed robber, I found the power to survive.

You can say,
"I had to sleep in my car,"
or
"Hey! I woke up in the
neighborhood of my choice."

Richard Stockton

Are you afraid that someday you'll be homeless? Let's fondle the fear even more; you'll be exposed to weather that could kill you and criminals who certainly will. Snap into action, move into your car, and you're not a vagrant; you'll always have a roof over your head. These are the advantages I found as a young performer:

- You won't get carsick; you'll get homesick.

- You can use resident-only parking.

- Smiling teenagers pass Happy Meals through your front door.

- Park on a main street, and you get six a.m. wakeup calls when your car is towed.

- You've got an excuse for beer cans on the back seat; you're drinking at home.

- You can travel when you are under house arrest.

For you men, living in your car is the perfect bachelor pad. No landlord. One utility bill. Windows in every wall, and you can get any view in the world you want. For outside maintenance, go through the car wash. For inside cleaning, roll the windows down and drive ninety miles an hour. As far as watching sports on TV; it is best done in bars where voluptuous women bring you beer. Women will have sex with you in your car, but they will not move in, and as long as you live in it, they will never bring up the subject of marriage. They will "need more space."

You can say,
"Our national debt is
money we've borrowed
from ourselves,"
or
"Hey! We don't have
to move."

Richard Stockton

Happiness is not an acquisition, but an ability we must master.

- Having paint and a brush does not make a confident painter, but it can be a wild time in a motel room.

- I have a house now, but I still love to sleep in my car. When I sleep in my car, I'm in the driver's seat. I've got direction. I wake up fully dressed, ready to go, with my foot on the gas.

Acquisition alone will not make you happy.

Driving in commuter traffic, I saw an apartment building banner that said, "If you lived here, you'd be home by now." I thought if I could have an apartment there, I'd be truly happy. As I got closer, I saw that the sign had bullet holes in it. I fondled the fear and instantly felt happy to be driving away from that neighborhood. As for the message on the banner, I thought, "I've got that by sleeping in my car. I'm always home."

You can say,
"My junk drawer is
so full it won't open,"
or
"Hey! My stuff is safe."

Richard Stockton

Fondling the Junk Drawer

The junk drawer is the perfect symbol of the fallacy of happiness by acquisition because it is your repository for hope, things of potential value, but that are not useful now. You may believe that a properly nurtured junk drawer will eventually save the day, that day when you will whip out a fat, blue broccoli rubber band and fix your glasses. Or you will have a specific need for dull scissors. Or during an earthquake you'll casually reach for your junk drawer flashlight that only shines while being shaken. You are coveting things that may someday be valuable.

Junk drawers begin when you make a drawer "the coupon drawer," starting with pieces of paper that may someday be valuable. Once you have set that frame, it makes perfect sense to put in pieces of string that could be tied together, then the sunglasses with lenses that fall out, an empty Pez dispenser, a lock with an unknown combination, a key that says Yale, the severed head of a troll doll, an out-of-state traffic ticket that you didn't deserve, but sense you should remain aware of, an invitation to the high school reunion of someone who stood you up, a list of ecological tips from Exxon, a coffee cake recipe from "Awake Magazine," pennies covered with gum, a yo-yo with no string, a button that says, "Betsy Ross Would Be Proud To Sew H. Ross Perot's Pants," the red rubber sucker to a snakebite kit, and a ruptured Whoopie Cushion. It's a hope chest. A Mutant Ninja Turtle action figure with no legs will someday be worth a fortune to someone who only has Ninja Turtle legs.

You can say,
"I glued my thumb and index
finger together,"
or
"Hey, I'm in touch
with myself."

Richard Stockton

You've framed your junk drawer as a safe for things potentially valuable, but did you ever find the blender lid in the junk drawer? Not until the glass cracks. Your junk drawer is the perfect symbol of material acquisition neurosis because believing that if you have enough stuff in there, every item will be used to fix every other item in there, is like believing that acquiring things will eventually fix your life. It's as if acquiring more stuff will become a perfect ecosystem and support us forever. That's the addictive power of material acquisition and junk drawers; you always need to get one more thing.

How do you reframe this neurosis? First, get the drawer closed. Push down the contents with your entire weight or close it halfway, then poke with karate chops until the stuff in front pushes up the stuff in the back. Whatever it takes, close it. It should be so full that it won't open. Hey! Burglar proof. No one can look at it, not even you. You have a full junk drawer, forever. You no longer need to fill up your life with junk.

What if you live in your car? In your car, the junk drawer is called the glove compartment.

You can say,
"I've been locked up as a
paranoid schizophrenic,"
or
"Hey! I'm committed!"

Richard Stockton

Know that love will grow in your life. I heard a little girl jumping rope to a rhyme about the man she was going to marry:

Rich man, poor man, beggar man, thief,
Doctor, lawyer, Indian chief.

At first I defensively (fearfully) yelled back:

Actress, heiress, social worker, nurse,
Marry a woman with money in her purse.

I reframed my thinking from reacting defensively to enjoying the excitement of a woman who loves me for what I am. Today, I love a woman who sings:

Motivator, poet, works comedy bars,
Give me that boy who sleeps in his car.

You can say, "Mad scientists will clone people," or "Hey! Thank God we're immortal."

Richard Stockton

The Power of Now

When you fondle the fear you invoke the Power of Now. Why is "now" important? Because it is here. It is easy to remember. Living now is how to experience the wonders that are your true destiny.

- You want to know what is on TV now.
- You want your coffee now.
- You want to get online now.
- You want your romantic urges satisfied now.

Happiness is only available to you when you live in the moment. If you're not happy now, you're not happy. Do you feel happy remembering when Bill Gates got a pie in the face? OK, bad example. Do you feel happy while anticipating a hot date with the sexiest person you're ever met? All right, really bad example. What kind of clock are you happy with, the broken one, or the one that says what time it is now? When do you choose to say, "Hey!"? You choose it now.

When we fear living now, we live in an unreal world of television images. When we fear living now, we live in our heads and abandon the real world for the symbolic.

- We annihilate Native American tribes and name cars after them.
- We destroy trees and name streets after them.
- We kill our emotions and name support groups after them.
- We ignore our prisons and name TV shows after them.

Remember, the rest of your life will be lived in the future; your current life is being lived now.

I could say,
"I won't finish my self-help book in time,"
or
"Hey! I can call it The Last-Minute Manager."

Richard Stockton

The Power of Sooner or Later

You may ask, "What about stuff I don't want to do? Or what if I want it now and can't have it now?" The Power of Now can sometimes include the eternal Power of Sooner or Later.

My neighbors risk heart attacks to shovel snow, but, hey, all snow melts, sooner or later.

This may appear contradictory to the Power of Now. Resolve this conflict by saying, "Now I will invoke the power of Sooner or Later." Sometimes your best decision will be to use time as a tool. It is based on a fundamental law of physical science:

Something will either happen sooner, or it will happen later.

Latinos may say, "Mañana;" young girls may say, "Whatever;" casting agents may say, "We'll call you;" even in a recording, the great Doris Day sings, "Que Sera Sera," but they all call upon the eternal Power of Sooner or Later. Have you ever found money on the ground? Hey, sooner or later you will find more (Maybe not the best retirement plan). Invoke the Power of Sooner or Later now.

FONDLING THE FEAR

Use the Power of Sooner or Later to put time on your side.

- Hey, in the last seven years, I've replaced every cell in my body.

- Hey, my life has been lived in perfect chronological order.

You can say,
"I'm destitute in this
freezing cabin,"
or
"Hey! I'll manufacture frozen
spring water on a stick,
Naturepops."

Richard Stockton

Embracing your fear will give you power, and fighting your fear will sabotage your effort. Fear of failure will insure your failure.

I witnessed this dynamic on an Amtrak train as it wound through the Cascade Mountains in Oregon. I shared a car in the golden morning light with a leather-faced cowboy and an elegantly beautiful, black woman in a business suit.

At 11:30 a.m. the dreamlike ambiance of our gently swaying car was shattered by a pinched, nasal voice, which crackled out of the speaker in the ceiling. "Attention, please. The dining car is closed. Do not come to the dining car yet. We will open for lunch at twelve noon. Please stand by for further announcements about the dining car."

At 11:50: "May I have your attention? May I have your attention, please? The dining car is not open yet. I will inform you when we will be ready to serve."

At 12:05: "I have an important announcement. We are not ready to serve lunch in the dining car. Repeat. The dining car is not ready yet. Please stand by for further announcements."

At 12:15: "Your attention, please. I'm sorry to inform you that the dining car is not yet open. We are having trouble getting ready for lunch. Sorry for this delay. Repeat. The diner is not open at this time."

At 12:25: "Attention all Amtrak passengers. I have an important announcement."

The woman in front of me looked at the speaker and moved her head from side to side like an Egyptian dancer. "Really, honey?"

You can say,
"I can't believe I still dine
and dash,"
or
"There is a free lunch;
I just have to run for it."

Richard Stockton

The cowboy across the aisle jerked his head up toward the speaker and through clenched teeth growled, "Shut up."

The sharp little voice crackled on. "The Amtrak dining car is now open for lunch. We offer coffee with each dinner. We offer two entrees today; pork loins and stuffed shells. Every table has its own window, no waiting or reservations needed. Lunch is now being served in the Amtrak dining car." I noticed that no one got up to go.

At 12:42: "May I have your attention, please? Give me your attention. The dining car is now open and waiting for you. We have decided to extend the dining car hours today, so if you want to come later, you may, and you can come now, as well. You may come twice, if you want. Seating is available. Don't forget the free coffee. See you soon."

I watched the woman in front of me put on her headphones without plugging them in. The cowboy took off his hat and put his denim jacket over his head.

At 1:00 the steward's voice returned. "Yes. This is the final announcement concerning the opening of the dining car. It's open. We opened for you. We have food and beverages and no waiting. We'll be here, and we'll remain open."

At 1:15 his voice shook with the desperation of a betrayed friend. "It's time to eat. Don't you people get hungry? That's why we're here. In the dining car." The speaker clicked off and we never heard from him again. Not one person passed through our car to go to the dining car.

An entire train chose to go hungry rather than take food from a desperate man. He would have done much better as a desperado.

At 1:30 the lilt of an older woman's voice, with a warm southern accent, came over the intercom, "Diner's open," and we all got up to go eat.

You can say,
"I feel disconnected from my children's music,"
or
"Hey! Fa shizzel, my nizzle."

Richard Stockton

"Now Fear This!"

Fear of Other Cultures

Dear Rich:

I am CEO of a major corporation, and I am having difficulty relating to many of my employees with inner city backgrounds. How can I develop a rapport with these younger people, who seem to speak a different language?

Sincerely,
Robert Settleman

Dear Robert:

You'd be surprised how many CEOs are afraid of hip-hop culture when they should embrace it with excitement. First, what would happen if you embraced hip-hop culture? You might be known as The Gangsta CEO. Instead of "touching base with your peers," you might start "sending shoutouts to your homies." The more you fondle your fear of hip-hop culture, the more excitement you bring to your business.

Yours truly,
Sticky Icky Dicky Bob

You can say,
"My employees speak a
different language,"
or,
"It's time for the Gangsta CEO
to represent."

Richard Stockton

FONDLING THE FEAR

- Give members of your company gangsta names. Call your corporate accountant "Busta Bean."

- When announcing the arrival of internal investigators, call them playa haters.

- Instead of "Call me at your convenience," say "Hit me up on your celli."

- Your legal department isn't "tenacious," it's "off the heezee fo shezee."

- For your office dress code, have all men roll up their left pant leg. On casual Friday, they roll it down.

- Instead of "Our communications division is efficient," say "It's off the hook."

- Instead of calling the project manager "an associate," call him "my dogg."

You can say,
"Everyone I know is a drunk,"
or,
"Hey! Alcoholics Unanimous."

Richard Stockton

Fear of Becoming a Loser

Dear Richard:

I'm afraid of failing. I'm writing a book about people who spend all their money on diet and exercise programs. I've maxed out my credit cards to write this book and can't stop worrying that the whole project will go bust.

Sincerely,
Stanley Collins

Dear Stanley:

You are never failing, you are rewriting. You fear failure only because you say so. Hey, what if this "failure" is just your rough draft? I have a friend who wanted to write a weight-loss book. As his bank account dipped lower the book became Lose Your Ass In A Big Way. He kept going, and finally wrote Derriere To Spare.

Yours truly,
Rich By Name

You could say,
"I'm out of work,"
or
"Hey, I am CEO of my
company,
most valuable employee,
and top producer,
all while being self-employed."

Richard Stockton

Fear of Your Job Interview

Dear Rich:
I get so frightened at job interviews that I develop an eye tic.
What can I do?
Sincerely,
Fred Morgan

Dear Fred:
Instead of being afraid of your job interview, get excited about it. First, what is the real fear here? The real fear is that you won't get the job. When you fondle the fear, you discover that it's not really important to you whether or not you get the job but that you maintain your sense of personal power. Explain how you'll never be late for work: you plan to sleep in your car behind the office. Now you are excited; he is afraid. Enjoy his eye tic.

Break your pattern of fear by making one job interview as wild as you can.
- Make a pizza on his desk.
- If he touches you, scream and crush a ketchup pack against your nose.
- Ask if you could turn on the heat and interview in your underwear.
- Ask him to apply lotion to your back.

Yours truly,
Rich With No Résumé

You can say,
"They fired me."
or
"Hey! I won't work under
these conditions."

Richard Stockton

Fear of Being Fired

Dear Richard:

I'm terrified of the prospect of getting fired. I'm losing sleep over this. What can I do?

Sincerely,
Mandy Wheeler

Dear Mandy:
If you are worried about your unstable work environment, decide first, what is the worst thing that could happen? You could get fired. Now, imagine that you've got no letter of recommendation, there is a cloud over your résumé, and getting hired anywhere becomes impossible. Hey, you're self-employed. The more you get fired the easier it gets, believe me. Every firing has been a gift of freedom for me and now it docs not bother me at all. Opening your termination letter will have all the excitement of opening your biggest birthday present. You've been released. Let this excitement power you to start working for your own dreams.

Truly yours,
Rich In Spare Time

You can say,
"I'm living beyond my means,"
or
"Hey! I'm stimulating the
economy."

Richard Stockton

Fondling the Fear

Fondle your fear into action.

• Maybe your career has hit the skids, and your phone is not ringing. Take action to get that phone ringing; have it connected. Next, mention to anyone that you need either a financial planner or insurance. Your phone will never stop ringing.

• Maybe you're afraid that you've let your body go. How do you reclaim your body? Do a pushup. One. Do it now. Now you've established that you are a person who works out. Wait exactly sixty seconds, and do another pushup. Now you are a person who works out regularly.

May you use the rags of ruin
to gird your loins.

You can say,
"As I age my face sags,"
or
"Hey! The illusion of a chin."

Richard Stockton

Fear of Getting Old

Dear Rich:

Aging terrifies me. I shake at the thought of all that goes along with growing old.

Yours from over the hill,
Paul Montgomery

Dear Paul:

Your hair will turn gray and doctors will bleed your bank account dry. Now, fondle these fears and be ninety-five for a day.

- Instead of saying, "I'm losing my youth," you say, "Gray hair goes with my business suit."

- Keep medical doctors away as you age by wearing a medic alert badge that says, "No insurance."

Be old now. Get a fake ID that says you're a senior citizen and receive the benefits now; cheap movie prices, compliments on how good you look for your age and an excuse for spacey driving.

Yours truly,
Rich In Health And Years

You can say,
"The brain is nothing more than a computer,"
or
"Hey! After I crash, I can wake up and work."

Richard Stockton

Computer Fear

Dear Richard:

I'm afraid of computers and have trouble remembering computer terms. Can you help?

Not technically yours,
Flo Weston

Dear Flo:

People fear computers because working with them is like learning a new language. Fondle the fear. Does the word microchip make you think of what's left at the bottom of a bag of Doritos? Does floppy disc sound like a bad back? Does log on mean building up a fire, to you? Make computer language part of your everyday life.

- Call your plastic eating utensils "software."

- Instead of lighter wines, use your "port."

- When pushing crosswalk buttons, double click.

- When you feel pain say, "Mega hertz!"

shutting down,
r

You can say,
"They're asking for the moon."
or
"Hey! Time to drop trou."

Richard Stockton

Fear of Being Naked

Dear Rich:

My wife says that I'm afraid of being naked. It's wrong to be naked, right?

Sincerely,
George Riley

Dear George,

If nakedness is wrong, I'm wrong right now. What do natives in National Geographic and people in the south of France have in common? They are naked. My wealthy clients rarely wear clothes on vacation. Remember:

- The happiest people on television are naked.

- Until you are happy naked you'll never be happy with clothes on.

- You'll never love others naked until you love yourself naked.

Fondling your nakedness,
Richard The Bottomless

You can say,
"Boys will be boys,"
or
"Finally, no cross-dressing."

Richard Stockton

Fear of Clothing

Dear Richard:

I am a male massage therapist and often have difficulty doing my best work because some of my clients refuse to take off their clothes for a massage. How can I do my best?

Wanting to be all that I can be,
Fred Ferguson

Dear Fred:

You can give great massages to the fully clothed; you simply must use lots of oil. Hey, you can claim that your massage will relax and waterproof.

Sincerely,
Richard "Squishy" Stockton

You can say,
"I'm a three-time divorcé,"
or
"Hey! I'm not afraid to
make a commitment."

Richard Stockton

Jump From The Frying Pan Into Desire

Fear of Men

Dear Richard:

I'm always afraid of first dates. How do I establish rapport with a man without studying sports facts and his beer preferences?

Sincerely yours,
Lucinda

Dear Lucinda:

A more direct way of developing rapport would be to mirror the way he holds his body and to pace his breathing.

- Slouch in your chair.

- Keep your legs spread wide apart and grunt frequently.

- Make up a pet name for your genitalia.

He's locked into your pace and will follow you anywhere. Discover the real moments with your partner; ask yourself, "Are we in the same room?"

Truly yours,
Rich In Rapport

You can say,
"She only wants me for sex,"
or
"Hey! She only wants me for sex."

Richard Stockton

Fear of Women

Dear Richard:

When I'm on a date, I cannot connect. How can I get in sync with her?

Yours,
Gordon Hamlin

Dear Gordon:

The real fear is that she won't have sex with you. You fear she'll say, "I can't relate to you." Fondle "relate" and mirror her body language and attitude.

- Flip your hair back.

- Cross your legs above the knees.

- Use a mirror to put on chap-stick.

- When another man walks by, roll your eyes.

You will be so connected she may wonder if you're gay.

Yours truly,
Richard "Yin Yang" Stockton

It's easier said than done,
unless you stutter.

You can say, "My wife has multiple personalities," or "Hey! A threesome."

Richard Stockton

Fondle #3

In which of the following sentences could you replace the word "fear" or "afraid" with the word "excitement" or "excited"?

1) I look with _____ upon my job termination.

2) I'm _____ that I have nothing to wear.

3) I'm _____ that my girlfriend might be bisexual.

Choose the perspectives that best Fondle The Fear.

I have overcome my fear of commitment by:

1) Not making any.

2) Keeping my options open.

3) Maybe one of the above.

I have no fear of procrastination because I know:

1) If a thing is worth doing now, it will be worth doing later.

2) With only two choices, I've got plenty of time to choose.

Bonus Chapter!

I could say,
"What possible advantage is there to being born in Bakersfield, California?"
or
"Hey! 230,000 people, six last names."

Richard Stockton

Bonus Chapter!

The point of this book is to get you to fondle the fear and spend your life in your own way. It's your way or their way. When you visualize how each moment moves you toward your goals, achieving them is inevitable. When you drive frantically and are completely lost, instead of panicking, say, "I'm not sure where I'm headed right now, but I'm making great time."

The best things in life are not things; they are your dreams, your excitement and your interpretation of it all. Moment to moment, reframing your perception will let you lead a life you determine, even how you relate to others. Go ice fishing with your new boss; maybe it'll break the ice.

You can say, "He's tooting his own horn," or "Hey! He's got a horn."

Body builders look in the mirror and focus on what they like about their body. In the gym, they stare so hard at the mirror that they crash into one another. Hey, it's their frame.

Fondling the fear lets you perform at your peak. You know everything is working in your favor when you're reframing the fright.

You can say,
"Dyslexia is making me crazy,"
or
"Hey! Don't happy, be worry."

Richard Stockton

If you want to receive your own career specific "Hey!", just e-mail me:

mail@richardstockton.com

There is no charge. Your possession of this book has made us Possibility Partners. Tell me your career, your dream and your fear and I will send you your own career-specific "Hey!" within three days, unless I am camping or in a sensory-deprivation tank.

Ride an exercise bike to fitness. Fondle The Fear, and ride The Golden Tricycle to your dream.

Believe in yourself.
You really do exist.

Index

A

acquisition 97
action 95, 124
afraid . . 81, 89, 95, 114, 117, 119, 123, 127, 129, 132, 134, 137
age 124,125
All-Bran 71
anger 89
anorexia 36
arsonist 33
artist 40
auto parts 69

B

Bakersfield 43, 138
banjo 27
bank 24, 25, 75, 29, 117, 125
banker's hours 92
being stalked 80
Bill Gates 31, 105
bills 53
bisexual 137
blood pressure, type 39, 81
body builders 143
Bonus Chapter 139
bowling team 52
brain 25, 31, 67, 69, 126
brassiere 65
break the ice 141
bungee 71
Bush, George W 85
business 57, 59, 61, 113, 125

C

Cadillac 76
California Natural. 67
California public education. 14
calls 53, 95
cars. 39, 59, 81, 93, 95, 97, 101, 103, 119
career dream. 57
catatonic 46
challenge. 51, 72, 73
change the words 51
channeling 75
chant. 75
chicken manure. 76
chin 124
chiropractor 89
choice. 94
claustrophobic 43
commitment 132, 137
community 18
commute. 53
computer. 126, 127
computer fear 127
conditioning 25, 29, 31
conference calls 53
convictions 41
counterfeiter 40
crazy. 50, 142
creative. 33
critic. 69
cross dressing 130

D

deaf 33
depression. 32

desire 79
destiny 105
detention. 87
dine and dash 110
directions 90
disconnected. 112
divorce 66, 132
doctors. 42, 103,125
dollars. 57, 61
Doris Day. 107
dream . . 25, 29, 31, 33, 39, 41, 43, 45, 51, 57, 58, 67, 141, 143
dreams and aspirations 47
dress to impress 65
drinking 72, 95
driving 81, 97, 125
dumpster. 71
dying 15
dyslexia 142

E

earthquake 15, 99
eat. 49, 71
economy. 122
Einstein 64
Elvis. 75
evangelist healer. 83, 157
excitement. 15, 31, 33, 53, 81, 87, 103, 113, 121, 137, 141

F

facts 28, 55, 133
faith 83, 157
fame. 45
family. 57

fat 36, 37
fear . . . 15, 25, 29, 39, 41, 43, 51, 55, 67, 69, 81, 83, 87, 89, 95,
. . . . 97, 105, 107, 113, 117, 119, 123, 127, 135, 137, 141, 143
fear mongers 85
fear of becoming a loser 113
fear of being naked 129
fear of clothing 131
fear of commitment 137
fear of getting old 125
fear of men 133
fear of other cultures 113
fear of women 135
fear of your job interview 119
feel richer 55, 65, 83
fired 51, 120, 121
fireman 33
first date 133
focus 341, 81, 143, 157
fondling the fear 27, 33, 39, 43, 45, 53, 55,
. . . . 65, 75, 99, 107,115, 124
frame 99, 143
Franklin Delano Roosevelt 31
free lunch 110
freeway . . . . 27, 81 (See highways)
furniture 55

G

generation 75
get lucky 61
glasses 33, 99
goals 141
Golden Tricycle 41, 143
gorilla suit 61
grocery shopping 53
ground zero 87
growing old 125
Guinness Book Of World Records 45

H

Hacky Sack. 55
happiness 97, 105
Hey!". 29, 49, 51, 55, 57, 67, 71, 143
highways 55
hip hop culture 113
hit the wall 82, 83
Hollywood 59
home. 57, 95, 97
horns 27
hot dogs 71
house 39, 55, 97

I

illusion 124
Indy 500. 81
insults. 68
insurance. 69, 123, 125
interpretation. 31, 67, 141

J

Jailhouse Rock 75
job . . . .
33, 43, 119, 137
job interview. 119
· jump off the roof. 69
junk drawer. 98, 99, 101

K

Karaoke 88
keys 52

L

latinos. 107
laugh 157
lawyers 42, 107
legs 66
Los Angeles 57
love. 97, 103, 129

M

manic depression 32
marriage 50
marry 103
massage 131
method 45
mirror 65, 133, 135, 143
Mississippi 14
momentum 27
money 31, 40, 55, 61, 69, 96, 103, 107, 117
motivational speaker. . . . . 69 (See jump off the roof)
motivator 103
multiple personalities 136
Mutant Ninja Turtle 99

N

naked 83, 129
nap 33, 77
national debt. 96

national TV. 57
Native Americans 105
Naturepops 109
negative 157
neural freeways. 67, 69
NeuroLinguistic Programing. 157
neurosis 101
Nietzsche 28

O

opportunity. 51, 57, 65, 81, 83

P

pace 133
parents 29
Pavlovian 25
peak performance.. 141
Pepsi Cola 73
pig lips 71
police 63, 67
positive 51, 57, 67, 81, 157
possibilities 41, 45, 55, 67, 95
possibility 57
pot 63
potential 99, 101
power 29, 31, 33, 41, 65, 67, 77, 101, 107, 119, 121, 157
Power of Now. 105, 107
Power of Sooner or Later 107
prison 18, 52, 53
prisons 105
procrastination 137
procrastinator 41
programmed 25, 27, 75
prospects 71

Q

Q-tips 75

R

rags of ruin 123
rapport 113, 133
real estate 66
rebel 41
reframe 101
reframing 141
Renaissance Man 41
resources 55
response 77
romantic urges 105
root canal 51
rubber sucker 99
Russians 87

S

Sacramento 87
scared 83
schizophrenic 20
self employed 113
self help 106
self-starter 33
sex 134, 135
shaking 15
skateboard 15
sombrero 65
spirit 81
spit wads 69
Steely Dan 89

stimulus and response 67
stutter 135
success 28, 31, 67
support groups 105
survival 87
sushi 71

T

television 129
The Cold War 87
The Golden "Hey!" 51, 67
The Power Of Now 107
The Power Of Sooner Or Later 109
therapy 50
Thermal Butter Box 39
Three Faces of Eve 62
time 25, 26, 49, 51, 53, 61, 81, 97, 105, 106, 107, 114, 132
ton of bricks 86
tornado 15
tuba players 57
TV . . . .
46, 47, 105

U

unconscious 75

V

vacation 42, 129
vandalism 63
vending machines 83
violence 89

W

weeds of fear 67
weight loss 117
Whoppie Cushion 99
wife 51, 75, 129, 136
Windham Hill 55
work 43, 59, 92, 118, 119, 120, 121, 126, 131
worry 142

About The Author

Richard Stockton claims to have been a feral child raised by Republicans; he looks like a cross between Ronald Reagan and Don Knotts. When Richard was young, his father instructed him in the power of being positive, "Don't be so damn negative." Richard's desire to become an evangelist healer was frustrated because he had no faith. By focusing on any benefit he saw in any situation, he managed to survive and frequently prosper as a musician, radio talk show host, and finally as a comedian. During a NeuroLinguistic Programing seminar, he found that the NLP tool of Reframing was exactly the empowerment technique he had been using all along, looking for the positive benefit in any event. Even though his speaking engagements focus on this powerful tool, it seems that everything he does makes people laugh at him.